Road Worrier: Poems of the Inner and Outer Landscape

poems by

Sandra Anfang

Finishing Line Press
Georgetown, Kentucky

Road Worrier: Poems of the Inner and Outer Landscape

ACKNOWLEDGMENTS

"Hasta Monteverde" appears in *Silver Birch Press*, 2015.
"Perseids" appears in *The Sand Canyon Review*, 2015.
"Painted Desert" appears in the *Sand Canyon Review*, 2015.
"Postcard Poem" appears in the *California Poets in the Schools (CPITS) Anthology*, 2015.
"Night Kayaking" appears in my chapbook, *Looking Glass Heart*, Finishing Line Press, 2016.
"Everest" won an Honorable Mention is the 2016 Ina Coolbrith Circle Poetry Contest.

Publisher: Leah Maines
Editor: Christen Kincaid
Cover Art: Sandra Anfang
Author Photo: Sandra Anfang
Cover Design: Elizabeth Maines McCleavy

Printed in the USA on acid-free paper.
Order online: www.finishinglinepress.com
also available on amazon.com

Author inquiries and mail orders:
Finishing Line Press
P. O. Box 1626
Georgetown, Kentucky 40324
U. S. A.

Table of Contents

*For my grandmother, Ruth Dorfman,
whose stories aroused my gypsy spirit*

Bedouin Wedding
—Tunis, Tunisia

She crowns the faded throne.
Her bones, hollow as kestrels',
settle light on satin cushions.
She has given everything for this moment.

Inshallah

At her feet, cross-legged drummers beam
thrumming their soul songs
in homage to her flight
from maiden to wife.

Women circumambulate
kneel, gaze heavenward
at her grace
in the face of so much change.

They are dreaming
a single dream
of the moment they'll step over
on their wedding day.

Inshallah

In the market
beckoned by a tattooed crone
I sleepwalk in my American raincoat
buttoned neck to knee.

Jeans sprout
from the southern hemisphere
against a hundred ten degrees
of separation.

We eat sugar wafers
sip at pomegranate tea
wonder what the groom is thinking now
on his own wedding throne.

I marvel at the string of uncles
queued outside the marriage tent
holding vigil, drinking toasts
awaiting the victory shout.

Spring Break 1970
—Ozark Mountains, Arkansas

It was 1970 and the world
inside my head
was about to open
like the Red Sea.

Three women friends and I
high-tailed it to the Ozarks
looking for a mountain, other lives
escape from the school of cram.

We pitched our tents on a soft bluff rise;
coyotes spun a song cocoon around us.
A man with a gun leapt from his scooter
threw his hands in the air, barked

I don't know what it is, but peace!
Seems he'd never seen a woman in jeans.
I had to do the math to calculate
what year it was.

We passed through two-lane
euphemisms for roads
festooned with signs that bled
Christ died for your sins.

I thought *Hot Springs*
was a sexual reference
linked somehow to the omnipresent mattresses
sprawling in pop-up roadside dumps.

We felt like aliens from planet Detroit
where students and professors toked together
on the diag, whisked back in time
to the dinosaur days of mud-brown Memphis.

In a dim-lit club
buffalo fish menu scrawled across the wall
dead eyes glared
from an algae-rimed tank.

An antique black man, scrimshaw-faced
pressed two quarters in my palm
wheeled me toward the juke box, whispered
Play something both you and me like, Baby.

Koster

—*Koster Hopewell Site, Kampsville, Illinois*

We dug our way
deep under Koster's pig farm.
At six a.m. the sun laughed, unabashed
knowing it would be 118 by noon.

Moving mountains of manure
disturbing potsherds, bones
charcoal, flint tips
exposing skeletons
thrown out with the trash—
teeth like diamonds
disappearing in the sun.
We smeared those grins with Vaseline
preserving what remained.

As we dug deeper
soil thickened
turned the texture of coarse sand.
Sometimes crudely
sometimes deftly, with a dental pick
we read the history of Illinois
emblazoned on the walls.
At thirty feet, a dog from 8,000 B.C.
cradled her pups in a fetal pose.

Time travelers
we journeyed to a place
where Jesus shouldered the oppressed
cut our teeth on bits
of chert, snail and corn
stood waist-deep in rivers, shaking basket sieves
in inner space.

Today we stand in the graveyard
lay our mother in the ground
among her own:
mother, father, husband, aunt—
a whole generation plowed under
that we might dance, unfettered, in our own time.

These Bones
—Koster Hopewell Site, Kampsville, Illinois

If it hadn't been for these bones
digging would have been merely an exercise
      in moving dirt   building muscle
cataloguing the history of Illinois
one shard at a time.

Down through the ages we dug
on a dream elevator
past rotting carcasses
the mute bodies of horses and pigs
in freeze-frame poses
down to the catacombs
      how would it feel to be caught in the maelstrom
as the plow turned us under?

If it hadn't been for these bones
we'd have continued dancing delicately around features
traded our shovels for probes
when the soil changed color.

If it hadn't been for these bones
we'd still be sending snails
to the carbon dating lab
swilling green beer in that clothesline backwater
learned who was sleeping with whom
at red-checkered tables in the This and That
over fried catfish baskets.

Artifacts were our talismans;
I remember the heft of a stone ax
      in my hand, the thrill of a plumb bob,
pictured the Hopewell lowering it into the river
to snare the same fish we de-boned at Sunday dinners.

If it hadn't been for these bones
I'd have done it all again:
        made the alchemic leap from soft city arms
to muscled grit
        tasted the sweat and curses
tedium and awe
held them in my teeth like gold
        testing for malleability.

Everything changed when the shovel grazed
        a texture unlike any I'd sensed before
soft yet solid
the holy grail of my nineteenth year
under my pendulous jaw.

The skeleton flashed an idiot grin
        sprawled among the rubbish
draped in drunkenness.

If it hadn't been for these bones
I'd have stopped carrying the worn notebook
from nineteen seventy-five,
stopped pulling life from the scene
like rabbits from a top hat
for my students
        with their impassive eyes
through the deep midden of years.

Painted Desert
—Arizona Badlands

I'm lying on a sandstone slab.
The early April sun has warmed it, like a giant hand.
The wall of heat is not yet upon us.

Eyelids flutter open, shut against the blinding ball of light.
Back wiggles into rock's undulations.
Sky at the horizon is a striped serape.
Colors do-si-do like eagle dancers.

The desert smells of succulence
potpourri of fungi, prickly pear—the real medicine.
The bitter bite of *nopal* on my tongue.

Roadrunner and vole scurry through low brush.
Tumbleweeds whirl across the landscape
like rolls of chicken wire, chased by the stiff breeze.
Rattlesnakes shake coils loose in crevices, marking time.

Ravens scour the sky, picking at clouds.
India ink spills from their wings to the desert floor
penning indelible poems.

A pair of coyotes
romp in the wash
heedless
of the torrents to come.

Alone on my rock I forsake loneliness.
The cottonwoods are my father,
the pastel bands of sky, my mother,
the javelina, my lover.

Night Light

— Superstition Range, Arizona

The black suede sky boasted pinpricks
sprigs of light
that rained like drops of blood
from church stigmata.

Tears of release clouded my view
silvered the moon's cheek, neoned the chaparral.
Jumping Cholla's needles flamed
the night you said you'd found
your true north in me.

I unpacked my calves
stood and stretched
strolled among Saguaro
glad to be cut down to size.

I shined a torch into heaven
looking for my self
but couldn't find it there.
Ocotillo with its bright fingers
led me back to you.

Together, with our bellies
we swept the ruddy earth.

Everest

—HBO Movie

I retreat into the cushions
of the leather couch
as the team fords a crevasse
on horizontal ladders
flimsy as dental floss.
I should know better
than to watch this stuff.
It's nearly midnight when
adrenaline grips me like an ardent lover.
I burrow like the cat in the lettuce patch
grab for roots, a climber who
stabs the heartless ground with stakes
sometimes finding purchase.
The world's an iceberg and
we've too little oxygen for squabbling
our breath consumed by life-and-death decisions:
who will travel up the mountain
who turn back?
We follow the rope banister, tilt downward
single file, knowing any moment
life can be whisked away.
The vague sun's an all-seeing eye,
a bald pate, borne in the arms of Sherpas
a beacon browning out in the swiveling fog.

Coincidence
—Superstition Range, Arizona

The ribbon of road wound through high desert hills.
Saguaros silhouetted against a *rebozo* sky
of honeydew and cantaloupe
snared the first stars.

Two couples on a mission—
a full moon desert hike.
Barrel Cacti's silver spurs
would guide us to her quickening.

The windowless panel van
Crazy Jim had filched
from the lab
slipped blithely off the asphalt.

Heeler and Collie flew to the rear
cushioned us as we slammed into them.
Tires free-fell off the edge
taking the oil slick's dare.

Time reversed itself
before my eyes
just like the Readers Digest had promised—
a short but sturdy life.

I mouthed goodbye
with gratitude
felt the roller coaster plunge;
no time for fear.

Blocked by a random stump
we charged to a halt.
Confusion
splayed its hand.

Scanning the barren sandstone bluff
wondering how to open the sun roof
(the side door, upended)
I gaped at the tailgate, now a tinfoil ball.

The wild mustangs of our limbs
climbed against gravity.
Night gathered its leaves,
salved our cheeks with dew.

Killing time
in the barefoot country bar
in cutoffs and a halter top
we laughed at our nakedness

while we waited
for the tow truck
the only other business
on this lonesome stretch of road.

Ursa Major

—Sequoia National Park, California

In the summer of '73 we climbed
eight miles up into the Sierras
hefting forty pounds on city frames
disowned to nine thousand feet of redwoods
and lakes that iced at dusk under fog blankets.

We camped with a guide who'd run away from his life
a heli-ski pilot who'd broken all his bones.
What more's there to lose? he asked.
It was the summer of "Cinnamon Girl" but we sang "Cinnamon Bear."

I wrote a letter to a man from camp
who doubted two city girls
could sling the western winds that way
pitch stuff sacks bear-proof-style each night
with humor if not grace.

Soaking lentils for a dinner stew
we passed the pipe
that signaled effort's end
guarded embers, watched aspen curls ignite.

A black bear tore through camp at breakneck speed
summoned as in a dream by the musk of mountain trout
carried on the wind from a neighbor's camp.
—Did you see that?
Our nodding heads drew Rorschach figures on the sky.

A few days later, during our descent—
the mountain having agreed to spit us out—
a mother and her cub stood, gorging berries
on either side of the trail.

Planted hard as granite
she pierced me with a stare that could split logs.
I froze, with eyes at forty-five
then took great pains to mime the wide loop
I would cut around them.

I held her gaze, chin tilted
down in deference.
Life turned, as it sometimes will,
on the tumbler of my heart.

To say that moment changed me is to rewrite
everything that happened next.
Half-mothered girls were girded
by the steam that issued from the great sow's tongue
a baptism that would outlive our lives.

I've seen that look in a thousand mothers' eyes:
this child eclipses all that came before.
Forty years down the trail I still think
about the runaway guide

wonder how he'd have turned out
had his afterbirth been licked
drop by precious drop
by a mama bear
like berry jam straight from the source.

Perseids

—American River, near Nevada City, CA

The decade has softened my feet
like old rock
returning to sand.
Ten summers since I slid, wobble-legged
along the sheep-shale ribbons you called trails,
perched high above the North Fork
like some dauntless hellion,
stuffing fingers in my ears
to muffle puerile fears.
Brazen by day,
my words cut on a razor strop
the glow of evening campfires
sobered gilded tongues, silenced hearts
and quelled illusions of despair.
Night's breast
pierced by raucous meteors
spelled out "Happy Birthday"
in the sky.

Polar Bear
—Arctic Circle

When the ghost bear came
he was asleep in his tent
pushing the iron water with his paddle of dreams
limbs circling like his dog's in full gallop
each bristle in his beard standing at attention.
Ice cracked out a code under the beast's leaden feet.
The bear stood its ground
stared at him from atop an ice floe
with its hard, black eye
and a mouth that belied its might.
Dazzled by a salmon's rainbow flank
it spied and mauled in seconds
'til an elk silhouette crossed its line of sight.
In and out of the current
from island to shore
bank to ice floe
it stalked the elk
all that afternoon
through the night
& into the next morning.
The man slumbered fitfully
paralyzed with cold and fright.
Should he load his camera or his gun?
Bear repellent stood just out of reach
but his hands were shackled
to his shell-shocked mind.
After two long days
the bear bested the elk
then made its getaway.
He loaded his canoe
and set off across the bay.

Plunge
—Banana Shout Cottages, Ocho Rios, Jamaica

Huts of woven straw crown an ocean cliff.
Each morning, Cleo, the fruit lady,
wakes us with her song:
ah-renge joos, sour-sop joos.
It filters through the gauzy curtain of my dreams.
In the outdoor kitchen,
we cobble together an *ackee* breakfast
stumble into swimsuits
take the short hike to the promontory.
It takes me days to find the nerve to jump.
I watch with envy as the others
throw a kiss to island skies
and drop like ninjas over the ledge.
The fall is fifteen, maybe twenty feet;
the more I ponder it
the more my feet are fused to stone.
When I relent, the jackknife of my life careens—
heart, gut, and head plunge together from the edge.
As I fall I calmly bid my breath goodbye.
The ocean welcomes me into its bed.
Later that week a Rastafarian
teaches me the scuba dive ballet.
We stand knee-deep in shallow water.
Under the umbrella of his beneficence
I take a second plunge.
Eating jerked chicken on the topless beach
I try to comprehend what I've just done
and learn I've used less air than anyone.
Such a foreign brand of letting go
from the tumbling of love or lust.
Toes lose their grip on the floorboards
body and senses tumbling
towards the vortex or the light,
whichever comes first.

Song of Salmon
—Trinity Alps, California

The song of salmon's
a symphony of sound.
Hear it in the tinny tremolo
of gravel-nestled eggs.
Bubbles seek the sky
chant *Om.*
Alevin suck life from yolk sacs
graduate to fry
to parr
& smolt.
Listen to the swish and slap
of muscled tails on river rocks,
the drumbeat of rapids
pummeling their flanks
in flashing sun.
Smolt begin their journey
navigate pelagic waters
to the Bering Sea,
thrive on salt
imbibing krill and plankton
growing pink flesh
singing silver scales
in morning light.
Returning to their natal beds
following ancestral smells
preparing for the great ascent,
their songs are stories
woven for the young
melodies spun on whitecaps
embroidered in the stars
as their mating cries
punctuate the frigid air.

I Hunger
—My Dreaming Chair

I hunger for Spain
like a pungent paella
her *rojos* and *saffrons*
cobblestone walls
Madrids and Bilbaos
riot of sculpture, Gaudi towers
even the bloodstains of Guernica.

In dreams I feel the scorch
of the bull's breath
hear the matador's victory cry.
I see my mother in shirtwaist and pumps
retelling the tale;
when he hands her the bull's ear
the petals of her lips swollen with flattery.

Oh, to be a flatbed stowaway
absorbing pothole curses
hunkered, wrapped
in arching plane tree robes
their fingertips reaching
across the *avenidas*
like God giving life to Adam.

Coming the beaches
I hunt your voice
under the bright *palapas*
your smile bleeding into sand.
I inhale the sizzle of garlic
from your frying pan
giving you away to the breeze.

Postcard Poem
—Yucatan Peninsula, Mexico

Dear Embryo,

I know you'd love Merida
with its 200-year-old houses,
jaguars and red macaws.
Every night workers scream their protests
in the park with its wrought-iron loveseats.
The spice market sizzles under mountains of
umber, rust, and saffron. Dad and I cruised
Isla Mujeres—the Isle of Women. Merchants
proffered rhinestone-encrusted scarab beetles
on tiny leashes, wearing false eyelashes.
A Capuchin monkey named Juanita
wrapped herself around my skull.
You kicked in protest when I climbed the pyramid
at Chichen Itza, but you loved the moped ride.
When you're on the other side I'll take you there.

Love,
Mom

Hasta Monteverde
—Puerto Viejo, Costa Rica, 2013

At seven a.m. we fill the narrow road;
valises carve patterns in congealed mud.
The bus glides in through steamy air
radio cycles through stations pumping
opera, Latin heartthrob, *rancheria*
through outsize speakers.
We veer out of town past the raw food bars
coconut stands, *pulperias*;
a cubist montage the size of a dollhouse kitchen
recedes in the rear-view mirror.

My son sleeps off last night's *cerveza*
reeking of garlic with a barf chaser.
The barkeep told him there's nothing
in Monteverde where we're headed;
no party, *nada* but the naked jungle.
I hold my tongue
though the weight of it breaks my biceps;
can't fault a twenty-two-year-old
flattered by a rummy hotelier
who offers a gig with all the free beer he can drink.

At the first stop an *empanada* lady glides
through the bus, steam rising from her plastic tub
an offering to the Virgen de Guadalupe.
The spiced *pati* perfume follows me down the aisle
like a spurned lover, flips a switch in my brain.
Five hundred *colones* buys *la alma de la cocina*:
a Costa Rican Madeleine.
A *federale* hops aboard, takes his time
each passport a cipher he must decode.
It's only 8:15 and he's got the day to fill.

He and the *pati* princess do-si-do to the door.
The music rises like an equatorial sun
as we roll on to San Jose
to be delivered to our next adventure.

Night Kayaking
—Tomales Bay, California, 2015

Winding through the bay in blackness
our paddles carve gyres in lucent water
necks arched to scan the constellations.
Greek names sit on my tongue like codices
sanctify the mystery of the dinoflagellates
teeming all around us.
The soul swells to such beauty
returns to elemental forms.
Alpha Cassiopeia is the breast,
Beta Cassiopeia, the hands,
names like wands to awaken the body of the heavens
rouse the heart
aerate the myths we were suckled on.
We watch our blades
strike the tinderbox of floating ink
serving sprays of silver sparks.
Our eyes ignite and hold;
a light both momentary and eternal.

Black Whales at Fort Bragg

(after a painting by Natalie Goldberg)
—Fort Bragg, Mendocino County, California

We awoke in the purple falling-down house
tumbled from dreams of rainbow's reach
that sliced the panes like spun glass shards
deep in the brow of Agate Beach.

The sky turned cantaloupe and gold
its profile burnished the window's blank face.
Fan Palms tossed their manes in spindrift mist;
children streamed from doorways like unspooled lace

marched to internal drums down to the pier
where three black Humpbacks out on tour
spuming and sounding in the air
towed a dying tugboat in to shore.

It is possible that things will not improve
that the rip cord of time will continue to fray;
why should we care when telephone wires
plait our hearts across the rain-kissed bay?

Behind the Canvas
—Tunitas Creek Road, near Half Moon Bay, California

The white barn devolves
droops under its own heft.
The tang of damp straw from the hayloft
shoots an arrow to my brain.

Paint chips gouged to milky blue
cling to the clapboard.
The wind's the culprit,
stealing frosting from yellow cake.

I see the family sitting down to Sunday supper
Grandma in her wire-rims
flowered apron with its flint-tip scorches,
Grandpa in his red suspenders.

Yellow-stained fingers
pluck tobacco from his beard.
Today they celebrate
the spoils of a fifty-year run.

Two ghostly Chevy's guard the silo
their windows blown out
anointed with the stench of crank case oil
the hardy blood that fuels their veins.

A breeze plays tag in the open spaces
Listen!
There's a song of woodwinds,
crickets sitting in on harmony.

Three strays strut outside the toothless fence.
If you close your eyes you can taste the scent of sulfur
from their new-laid eggs
a mile downstream.

Blue Willow

—Salinas, California
(after the book by Doris Gates, © 1940)

I'd clutch the book as tightly
as Janey held the willow plate
arms married to its maternal roundness.

The only thing she owned
that had no function
aside from loveliness

it couldn't sweep the house
or shield her bony frame
against the August heat or January ice.

The elder child of Okies
who followed the harvest:
grape, almond, peach

she kept her heart latched
against the dare of friends,
excess love for one-room cabins

or verdant valleys rolling
beneath a gibbous moon.
She tended her baby sister

as well as any mother
had deep thinks
memorized the chant of crickets

queuing on September nights.
I craved the cleanness of her life
the dignity of her family's poverty

the hugeness of her waxing,
waning heart, its elegant armature
bolder than Orion in the blackest sky.

As I dunked my Oreos
twisted buttons on the Magnavox
I mourned my uneventful life

cluttered with suburban wiles
and dreamed of hugging
a single thing of beauty I could call my own.

The Meadow on Awakening
—Pt. Reyes National Seashore, Inverness, California

Light mounts the roofline
a thief on nimble feet;
the windows pastel,
pool with dew.

I unzip the nylon bag of sleep
feel the chill on every goose-fleshed limb
sleepwalk from my bed
                    each cell yearning for sun.

opening the cabin door
a velvet net of birdsong
defines the boundaries of my world.

dew glitters
twists off a railing;
                    a genie rises from a lamp.

silvered brush considers stirring
thinks better of it;
Monterey Pines stand at attention
reverent in their pews.

the soft complaint of quail crescendos
joins the chitter of songbirds
at their ablutions.

across the creek a raven's cry
slashes
            the somnolent sky.

Sandra **Anfang** is an award-winning Northern California teacher, poet, and visual artist. She is the author of four poetry collections and several chapbooks. Her poems have appeared in numerous journals, including *Poetalk, San Francisco Peace and Hope, West Trestle Review,* two *Healdsburg Literary Guild* anthologies, *The Tower Journal, The We'Moon Datebook* (2016 and 2017), *Rattle,* and *Spillway.* Sandra's chapbook, *Looking Glass Heart,* was published by Finishing Line Press in early 2016. She was a featured reader at the 2017 Petaluma Poetry Walk and Chair of the 2017 Ina Coolbrith Circle Poetry Contest. Sandra is the founder and host of the monthly poetry series, Rivertown Poets, in Petaluma, California, and a California Poet/Teacher in the Schools. To write, for her, is to breathe.

www.ingramcontent.com/pod-product-compliance
Lightning Source LLC
LaVergne TN
LVHW051614080426
835510LV00020B/3286